Mandala Coloring Book for Adults & Teens

150 Mandalas

Relieve stress and anxiety through creative art
Vol. II

by
Marianne Jacobsen

Leave a 1-Click review, please!

I would be incredibly thankful if you could just take a few moments to leave a review when you are ready. To make it easier, I have included a QR code below for you to scan with your camera on your phone, which will take you straight to the Amazon review page.
Thank you in advance.

Best regards, Marianne Jacobsen

Scan this
if you are in the USA:

Scan this
if you are in the UK:

23

31

44

63

99

Made in the USA
Columbia, SC
26 November 2024